My Heart Hurts

by
Karen Jaggers, LPC

This book is dedicated to
helping all the broken hearts
learn to heal

My Heart Hurts .... A Grief Workbook for Children

For information contact:

Karen Jaggers, LPC

kjaggers@thejaggersgroup.com

www.thejaggersgroup.com

Life is like a flower...
there are many seasons to our life

- The flower begins to grow from a small seed
- Soon it is full of color and loves the sunshine
- Eventually its time on earth comes to an end

Can you draw the stages of the flower?

People go through life stages too...

- First we are born, and then we begin to grow
- We do lots of fun things and meet lots of people
- But just like the flower, our bodies won't last forever
- There comes a time when our body's time on earth is over
- Can you draw pictures of people at different ages?

Sometimes the **people** we care about aren't **able** to be here anymore......

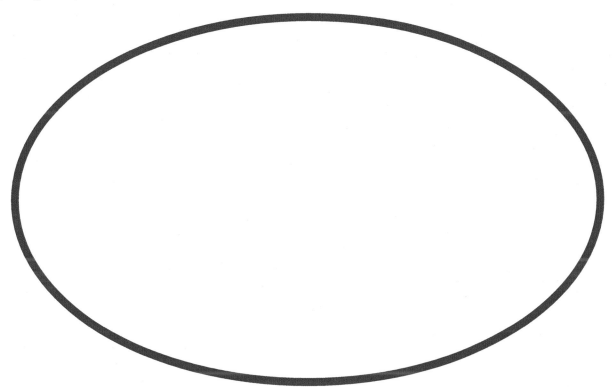

Draw a picture of the person you are missing

When a **person** dies, it means that

their **body** doesn't work anymore....

There are lots of reasons people die....

Draw some ways people can die....

Even though their body is gone forever from our lives, they are not in any pain and they are not afraid.

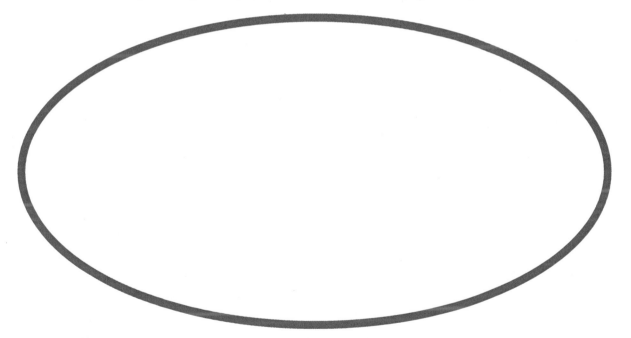

Draw a picture of the person you are missing doing something they enjoyed doing.

I'm sure you miss them very much....

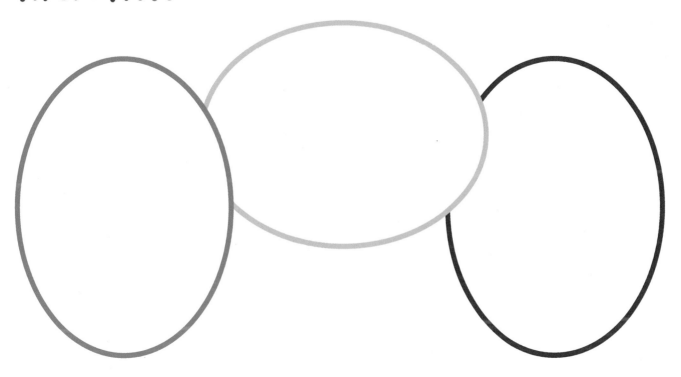

Draw pictures of the emotions you are feeling.

Sometimes you might worry that you will forget the person who has died, but that will never happen.

Can you draw a happy memory of you and the person you are missing?

Sometimes you will miss them and feel very sad.

But they will always be in your memories forever....

Although their body is gone,

their spirit will live on forever

in another place.

Their spirit is going to a new place and no longer needs their body. That is why we have a funeral.....to say goodbye to the body and to wish the spirit happy travels as it continues on to a new adventure!

No matter how much you miss someone who has died, there is no amount of wishing that will bring them back......

They have already begun a new adventure!

If you are mad or sad or angry.....those are normal feelings to have when you lose someone you love.

Draw a picture of how you are feeling today.....

Just like missing someone

cannot bring them back,

your thoughts or feelings

cannot cause someone

to die......

It is normal to feel sad when someone you love dies.

It is normal to feel confused or mad, too.

Sometimes you think that there might be something you can do to bring them back, but there is not.

Then sometimes, you may not feel sad or mad at all.

And that is okay, too.

It may take some time for your brain to understand that the person is really gone.

No one knows exactly what happens when we die. Some people believe we go to Heaven. Some people believe our life starts anew here on earth, just like the flower.

Draw a picture of what you think happens when a person dies.

Sometimes your body will physically hurt because you miss someone so much.....

Color areas of your body that have been hurting......

There are things we can do to help when our body hurts......

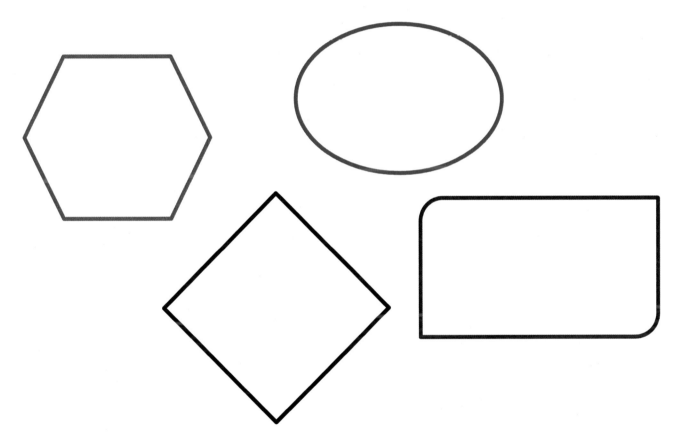

What are some things you can do to make yourself feel better?

Sometimes people feel scared or worried about things when someone dies......

Draw or write the things that you are scared or worried about

Even though you are sad, you will not be sad forever......

you will always remember this person,

but someday when you think of them you won't feel sad;

you will remember happy things....

47

Draw how you are feeling today

There are lots of people who care about you and are here to talk to if you are feeling sad.....

Who can you talk to when you are feeling sad? Write their names in the stars.

Even though you are sad, there are still happy things in your life.....

Draw pictures or lists of things
that make you happy!

You may feel different after this has happened, but you are still you!

What are some interesting things about you?

It's important to remember that there are lots of people who love and care for you....

Draw or list some of these people

If you feel very sad, there are lots of people who you can talk to ANY time you need to.

Even if it's in the middle of the night...
or in the middle of school...

someone will always be there for you.

Write down the names and cell numbers of three people who you can call if you are having a very bad day

_____

_____

_____

_____

_____

_____

What makes you feel better when you are feeling sad?

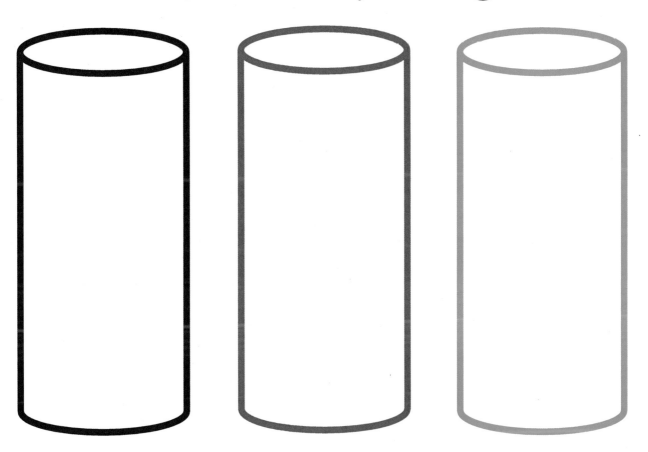

Draw or list things you can do to help you feel better

Trying to think of how things could have been different if only this hadn't happened only makes you sad.
Its called

Magical Thinking

But no one can change what has already happened.

No amount of
    wishing,
        bargaining,
            or hoping.....
Can change what has
        happened.

There **are** lots of people who love and care about **me**......

People from my family:

People from my school:

Other friends and pets:

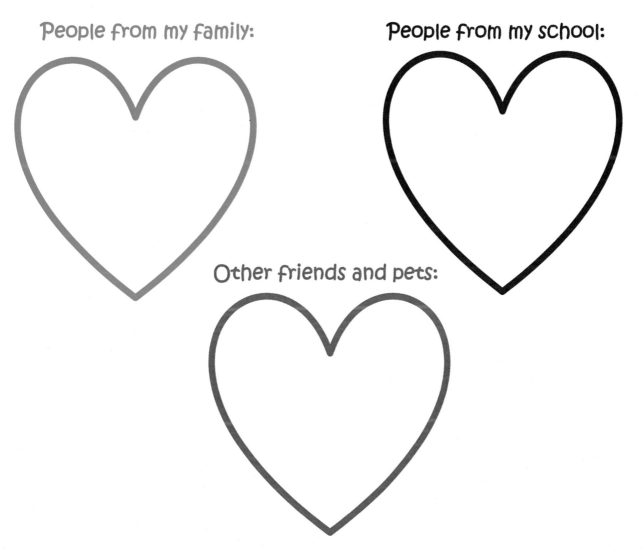

You may have met lots of people who knew your loved one and want to tell you how  much they meant to them. You may have met them at the funeral, or received cards or flowers from them.

Death is a natural part of life.

The person who is gone would not want you to be sad all the time.

They would want you to be happy when you think of them.

Sometimes it helps a lot to write a letter to the person you are missing!

Dear: _____

_____

_____

_____

_____

_____

_____

Love,

Even though they are gone from us physically, their love will always be with you. They will love you forever.

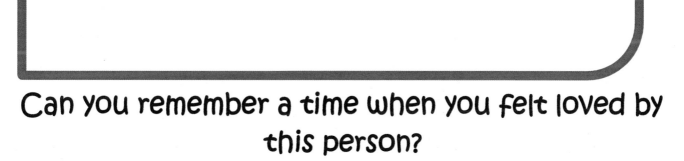

Can you remember a time when you felt loved by this person?

Now is a sad time, but there were happy times too, and you can always remember those times to help you feel close to the person who has died.

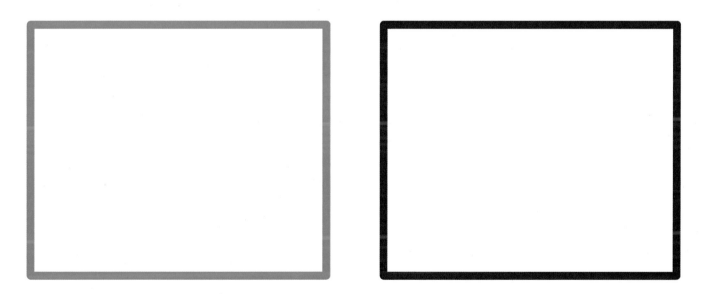

Can you remember some happy or funny times?

Some things that I will always remember are...

Losing someone you love is sad, but that doesn't mean you can't be happy about other things at the same time.

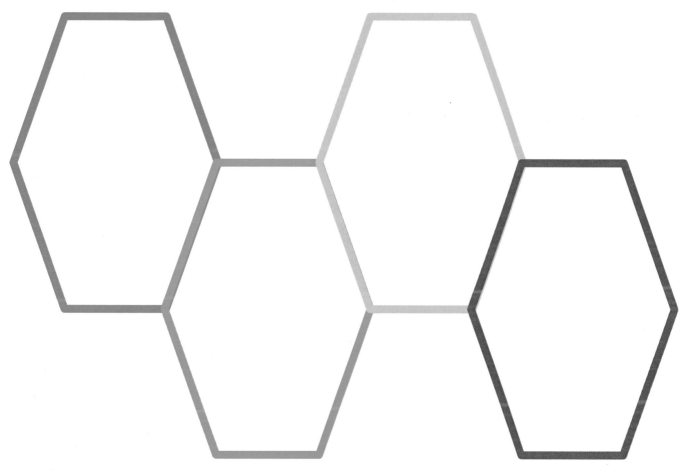

What are some happy things?

You may have lots of questions about what happened to your loved one. It's okay to ask questions......

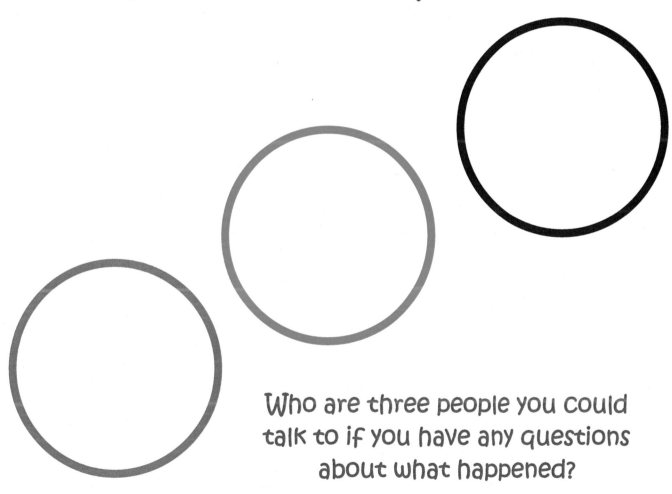

Who are three people you could talk to if you have any questions about what happened?

One day **you will feel** happy again.......

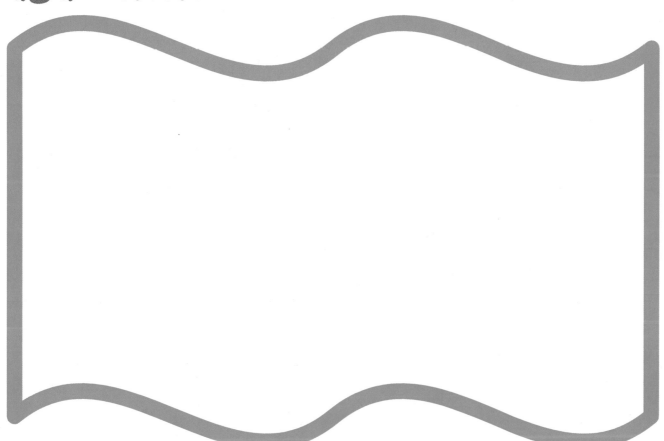

Draw a picture of you in the future being happy!

Sometimes, when you lose someone who is important to you, you may also worry about losing other people. There are lots of people who love you. There will always be lots of people who will help take care of you so that you will not ever be alone. Some of these people are:

_____

_____

_____

_____

You may notice that school feels different now. It's okay if you are still sad. You may have trouble concentrating or remembering things because you are sad. This happens to lots of kids but not everyone.

List three people who you could go to if you were sad at school....

1. _____

2. _____

3. _____

If you feel like you are having a very hard time and feeling very, very sad you need to tell your parents and your teachers.

They will understand and be able to help you feel better.

People I can talk to if I am sad
at SCHOOL ...

_____

_____

_____

_____

People I can talk to if I am sad
OUTSIDE OF SCHOOL ...

_____

_____

_____

_____

It's important to remember that it's okay that your heart hurts sometimes.

You loved this person and miss this person very much.

Your heart hurts so much because you loved this person so much.

Here is a great trick to help you feel better when you miss your special person.

Put your hand over your heart. Can you feel it beating?

Remember, those we love will live on forever in our hearts....

So, when you feel that heartbeat, you can remember that your loved one is always right there with you in your heart!

You might want to do something to remember your loved one.
Talk to your family and discuss what you could do to remember your loved one.

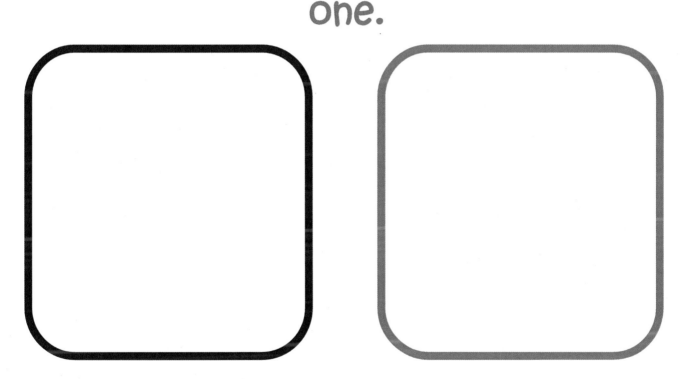

Write or draw some ideas of what you could do....

Sometimes you will miss this person and wish you could talk to them again.

You can talk to them anytime you want, but they won't be able to talk back to you.

You can talk out loud or you can talk to them inside your head.

If you want to feel close to them, you can think of a favorite activity you did with them or that they liked.

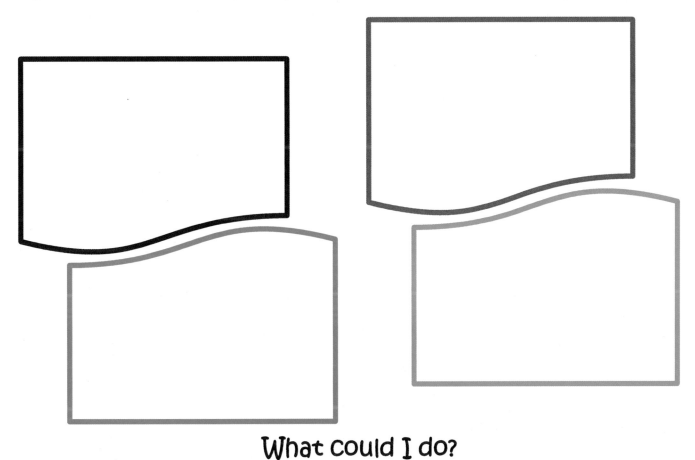

What could I do?

Ask your family for a picture of your loved one so that you can put it on this page to look at any time you want.....

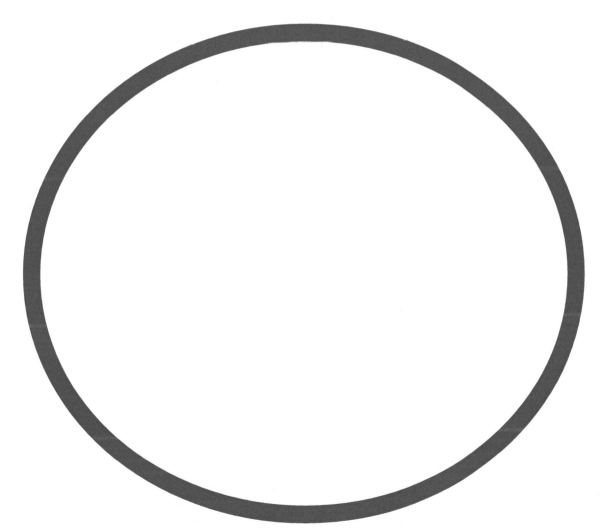

Made in the USA
Las Vegas, NV
20 April 2024

88933032R00067